BODY ART

SPECIAL THANKS TO

Tiki (Kristina) Rand
designer, exhibitions division
australian museum
TIKI DESIGNED THE EXHIBITION GRAPHICS AND HAS
CONTRIBUTED TO THE OVERALL PUBLICATION OF
THIS BOOK.

Trish McDonald
chair, body art project team
australian museum
TRISH HAS OVERSEEN THE RESEARCH AND DEVELOPMENT
OF THE BODY ART PROJECT SINCE ITS INCEPTION.

Leanne Brass
archaeological collections officer
anthropology division, australian museum
LEANNE WAS RESPONSIBLE FOR DEVELOPING THE
CONTENT OF THE BODY ART EXHIBITION.

BOOK DESIGN BY STUDIO CPM, UTILISING EXHIBITION
LAYOUTS DESIGNED BY TIKI (KRISTINA) RAND.